LEGO

Super Nature

Written by Rona Skene

Penguin
Random
House

Senior Editor Laura Palosuo
Senior Designer Anna Formanek
US Editor Megan Douglass
Designer James McKeag
Editorial Assistant Nicole Reynolds
Production Editor Siu Yin Chan
Senior Controller Lloyd Robertson
Managing Editor Paula Regan
Managing Art Editor Jo Connor
Publishing Director Mark Searle

Inspirational models designed and created by
Jason Briscoe, Nate Dias, and Jessica Farrell
Nature consultant Cathriona Hickey
Photography by Gary Ombler

Dorling Kindersley would like to thank Randi Sørensen, Heidi K.
Jensen, Paul Hansford, Martin Leighton Lindhardt, Charlotte
Neidhardt, Henk van der Does, and Nina Koopmann at the
LEGO Group. Also, at DK, Beth Davies for additional text;
Nicole Reynolds and Lisa Stock for editorial assistance;
and Julia March for proofreading and index.

First American Edition, 2021
Published in the United States by DK Publishing
1450 Broadway, Suite 801, New York, NY 10018

21 22 23 24 25 10 9 8 7 6 5 4 3 2 1
001–321869–July/2021
Page design copyright ©2021 Dorling Kindersley Limited

LEGO, the LEGO logo, the Minifigure,
and the Brick and Knob configurations
are trademarks of the LEGO Group.
©2021 The LEGO Group.

Manufactured by Dorling Kindersley, One Embassy
Gardens, 8 Viaduct Gardens, London SW11 7BW,
under license from the LEGO Group.

A catalog record for this book is available
from the Library of Congress.

ISBN: 978-0-7440-2857-7
Library ISBN: 978-0-7440-3842-2

Printed and bound in China

For the curious

www.LEGO.com
www.dk.com

MIX
Paper from
responsible sources
FSC™ C018179

This book was made with Forest
Stewardship Council ™ certified
paper—one small step in DK's
commitment to a sustainable future.
For more information go to
www.dk.com/our-green-pledge

Contents

Tree of life

Almost two million animal species belong to the same huge family—the animal kingdom. Animals come in so many shapes and sizes because over millions of years they have adapted, or changed, to survive better in different environments.

Odd-toed hoofed mammals

Ocelot

Carnivores

Pangolins

Primates

Red howler monkey

Rabbits

Arctic hare

Rodents

Marsupials

Dormouse

Reptiles

Reptiles have tough, scaly skin. They need to sit out in the sun to keep their bodies warm.

Lizards and snakes

Turtles and tortoises

Desert tortoise

Crocodiles

Horned viper

Yacare caiman

Sharks

Bony fish

Angelfish

Birds

Scarlet macaw

Birds

There are about 10,000 types of birds, and all of them have feathers. They have wings, too, but not all birds can fly.

Rays

Spotted eagle ray

Fish

Fish have special features for life underwater. Most have waterproof scales, and fins that help them swim.

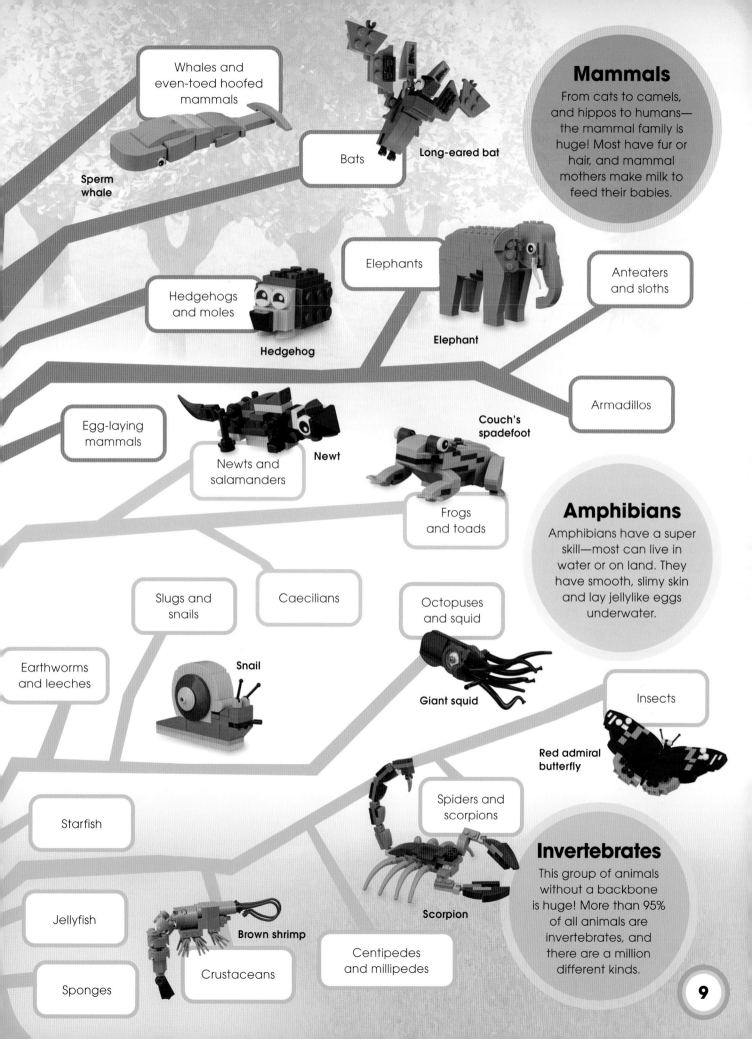

Whales and even-toed hoofed mammals

Sperm whale

Bats

Long-eared bat

Mammals

From cats to camels, and hippos to humans—the mammal family is huge! Most have fur or hair, and mammal mothers make milk to feed their babies.

Elephants

Elephant

Hedgehogs and moles

Hedgehog

Anteaters and sloths

Armadillos

Egg-laying mammals

Newts and salamanders

Newt

Couch's spadefoot

Frogs and toads

Amphibians

Amphibians have a super skill—most can live in water or on land. They have smooth, slimy skin and lay jellylike eggs underwater.

Slugs and snails

Caecilians

Octopuses and squid

Earthworms and leeches

Snail

Giant squid

Insects

Red admiral butterfly

Starfish

Spiders and scorpions

Jellyfish

Brown shrimp

Scorpion

Invertebrates

This group of animals without a backbone is huge! More than 95% of all animals are invertebrates, and there are a million different kinds.

Crustaceans

Centipedes and millipedes

Sponges

9

Polar bear

Narwhal

Orca

Wandering albatross

Salmon

Water and ice

More than two-thirds of the Earth's surface is covered in water or ice. All over our blue planet, water is home to all kinds of animals and plants.

Water and ice habitats

Watery habitats can be warm or cold, fast-flowing or still, sunny and shallow or dark and deep. Whatever the type, all of them are bursting with life.

◀ Rivers

Rivers attract different animals and plants depending on how deep or fast-flowing the water is. Rivers are also superhighways that allow living things to move between habitats.

▼ Ponds

Ponds can be in the country, parks, or even in your backyard! They're perfect for plants and animals that don't like the hectic swirl of life in moving water.

Swamps and wetlands ▲

When a mighty river bursts its banks and spills onto the land, it creates a vast swamp—a unique habitat that's a mixture of both water and land.

▲ Coral reefs

A coral reef is a dazzling undersea garden with a rainbow of shimmering colors. Warm water, plenty to eat, and shelter from the waves also make it a brilliant habitat.

▼ Beaches and rock pools

The ocean is big, deep, and full of danger, so some smaller sea creatures prefer to hang out by a shallow beach or in a safe, sun-warmed rock pool.

▲ Ocean depths

Some sea creatures scoot around on the sunlit surface of the ocean, while others lurk thousands of feet below in the deepest, darkest depths.

▼ Polar regions

At the extreme northern and southern points on Earth, it's either cold—or really, really cold! Only the best-adapted animals and plants can survive this frozen world.

▲ Frozen tundra

In such a chilly and windswept place, you have to keep out the cold to survive. For tundra wildlife, layers of super-thick fur or feathers are essential.

Flowing rivers

Rivers provide plenty of something that all living things need to survive—fresh water. In North America, from clear, fast-flowing mountain streams to wide, muddy, slow-moving waterways, the river means home sweet home to many different animals and plants.

▼ Dragonfly

Dragonflies zoom over rivers and lakes, moving expertly in all directions and even hovering in place like helicopters. They never move far from the water as it's where the females lay their eggs.

Can fly forward and backward

Can see in many directions at once

Thick, dark brown fur with light-colored tips

Grizzly bears have a very good sense of smell

I CAN SEE DINNER SWIMMING NEARBY.

Long, strong claws make it good at climbing trees

▲ Grizzly bear

In summer, the grizzly bear stands for hours by a small waterfall, patiently waiting for its favorite food. Then, with a sudden snap of its mighty jaws, it seizes a salmon that is leaping upstream.

Bear head

The grizzly's head is made up of several layers. It attaches to two jumper plates in the bear's neck.

Face built on 2x3 plate

1x1 brick

1x2 tile

1x2 jumper plate

Middle layer links face and top of head

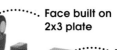

Build it!

◄ Willow tree

Willows are important riverside trees. Their huge, strong roots strengthen the riverbank, stopping soil from crumbling away. They also suck up lots of water, preventing flooding when river levels rise.

Drooping branches often trail in the water

Tail tale

The beaver's powerful tail is a 1x2 plate with bar with a 2x2 wedge plate with tab attached to the end.

Build it!

········· 1x2 plate with bar

2x2 wedge plate with raised tab

1x2 jumper plate

I CAN CHOP DOWN A SMALL TREE IN FIVE MINUTES!

Yellow teeth contain iron ······

North American beaver ►

Beavers are always busy building! With their strong teeth they gnaw though trees, using them to build a dam in a river. The dam creates a pond, where the beavers can build a cozy home called a lodge.

Strong, flat tail powers the beaver through the water

····· **Waterproof fur**

HOPE THAT GRIZZLY BEAR DOESN'T NOTICE ME!

Silver fin

Color changes from silver to red during the swim home

Salmon ▲

Salmon spend most of their lives on the move. Soon after they hatch, they head off to live in the sea. Then when they are grown, they make the long, exhausting trip back to their home river to have their young.

Habitat facts

Rivers are made of **fresh water**—they are not salty, like the sea. A river starts as **a tiny stream** of rainwater or melted snow, which flows down from hills or mountains, **growing bigger** or joining other rivers until it reaches the sea.

15

Tranquil ponds

Even the smallest pond is an amazing habitat, bursting with life. Most ponds are not very deep, so sunlight can reach to the bottom. This means lots of plants can grow, providing food, oxygen, and shelter for many different animals.

The flower is made up of a fuzzy lower part topped with a spike ......

Tall, thin leaves

Cattail ▶

Cattails grow in thick clumps at the water's edge. They are a vital part of the pond habitat, with all kinds of animals using them for shelter and food.

▼ Newt

Newts hatch from their eggs underwater, but spend most of their lives on the land. In spring, they plop back into the pond to breed and lay their eggs.

Narrow, lizard-like snout

Bright belly warns off enemies

I CAN WALK ON LAND AND ON THE BOTTOM OF PONDS, TOO!

Newt look

A plate with clip attached to a plate with bar makes a movable neck for the lizard. Its head is a brick with four side studs.

1x1 plate with clip

1x1 brick with four side studs

Plate with tooth forms bottom of snout

Build it!

Goose build

Bricks with one side stud form a central hub to which the goose's wings and chest are attached.

Build it!

..... Stacked angle plates make layered wings

Feet are minifigure flippers .....

Habitat facts

Some **pond insects** have adapted to **walk on water**! The waterproof hairs on a **pond skater's** feet trap tiny air bubbles, meaning it can **run** over the water's surface on its own **cushion of air**!

I ALWAYS TRAVEL SOMEWHERE WARMER FOR THE WINTER.

Water vole ▼

This shy rodent digs its burrow in the banks of a pond or river. Its strong front teeth are ideal for gnawing tree bark and thick reeds.

I LOVE A NICE, CHEWY CATTAIL FOR BREAKFAST!

Webbed feet make swimming easy

▲ Goose

In winter, flocks of geese from the Arctic make the pond their home. It's much warmer, and there's plenty of grass and pondweed for everyone!

Brown fur is perfect camouflage for muddy ponds. .....

..... Strong claws make good diggers

◄ Water lily

This plant's long stems mean its flowers and leaves can float on the pond's surface and soak up the sun's energy.

Scented flowers attract insects, which spread pollen .

..... Stems grow from the pond's muddy bed

Swamps and wetlands

South America is full of soggy, boggy swamps, called wetlands. The Pantanal is the biggest wetland in the world, covering parts of Brazil, Paraguay, and Bolivia. With its lush plant life, it's a food-filled home to an amazing 10,000 different animal species.

Pink band turns red when the jabiru is on high alert

Grows to 4 ft 11 in (1.5 m) tall

Habitat facts

What do you need for a wetland habitat? **Water**, of course, and lots of it! In the Pantanal's **rainy season**, so much rain falls that more than 80% of the land is **underwater**. In the short dry season, the ground doesn't get a chance to dry out properly before it starts **raining** all over again.

▲ Jabiru stork

This lanky creature is the biggest flying bird in South America. It strides through the shallow waters, dipping in its long beak to feed on fish and frogs.

I SPY WITH MY BIG EYE ... DANGER!

Big eyes to spot prey in murky water

Water hyacinth ▼

These fast-growing plants drift wherever the water takes them, trailing their roots behind them. Local people weave their thick stems to make baskets.

Flowers produce food for long-tongued bees and hummingbirds

▲ Red-bellied piranha

Fearsome and fast, this fish has mighty jaw muscles and flesh-ripping teeth. A pack of hungry piranhas can devour a whole cow in minutes!

Giant lily pads

Angle plates hold up this enormous lily pad's curving sides. The flower is attached with a 1x4 plate.

1x2/1x2 angle plate

1x4 plate

1x2 curved slope

Build it!

▼ Giant water lily

The huge, round leaves of this plant are so wide and strong that you could sit on one! These floating saucers provide a handy resting place for frogs and insects.

The giant lily has a small, white flower

Leaves connect to a thick stem growing from the river bottom

Hidden spikes under the leaves stop fish from eating the plant

MMM, PIRANHA! MY FAVORITE SNACK!

Eyes on top of head so it can see while the rest of its body hides underwater

Tough, bony scales along back

Between 70 and 82 sharp teeth

Yacare caiman ▲

This member of the alligator family likes to cruise along on a mat of floating plants. It snuffles out river snails and cracks their shells with super-sharp, cone-shaped teeth.

Head build

The caiman's eyes attach to plates with light clips. A plate with clips and a plate with bar make a hinge for its chomping jaws.

Plate with light clip

Tooth pieces attach to plates with clips

Build it!

Ocean depths

An ocean might seem like a single huge habitat, but it's actually made up of different zones—from the sunlit, warm waters near the surface to the deepest, darkest trenches. Although some residents can live at different depths, most are best adapted to one zone, and stay within its limits.

Atlantic bluefin tuna ▼

The big, strong bluefin is a top hunter in the sunlit zone. It's one of the speediest fish in the world, zipping through the water at speeds of 43 mph (70 kph)!

Powerful tail

Streamlined body

Bulging eyes help it spot prey

◄ Hatchet fish

In the twilight zone, this fish has a clever way of hiding from danger. Light organs on its belly and tail shine downward, making the fish harder to spot from below against the dim sunlight.

THESE LIGHTS ARE HANDY WHEN I DROP MY LUNCH, TOO!

I SPEED ALONG BY SUCKING UP WATER AND SQUIRTING IT OUT.

Eight shorter arms and two long tentacles for grabbing food

Huge eyes

▲ Giant squid

This secretive, bus-size monster has the biggest eyes in nature for seeing in the deep, dark waters. It has fierce undersea battles with sperm whales!

◀ Orca

Sometimes called killer whales, orcas are actually giant dolphins. These clever hunters work together to catch seals or shoals of fish.

Strong flippers to power through the water .....

WHERE'D THAT SQUID GO? HE WAS HERE A MINUTE AGO!

▼ Sperm whale

This huge whale is the world's biggest hunter, or predator. It can dive very deep, where it uses sound waves to hunt for giant squid in the pitch-black waters.

Habitat facts

The ocean is divided into three main zones:
Sunlit zone These warm waters are full of light and bursting with animal and plant life.
Twilight zone This region gets darker and colder the deeper you go. No plants or seaweed grow in this zone, so animals need to hunt other creatures to survive.
Dark zone At the lowest depths, it's seriously cold and totally dark. Only a few super-adapted animals can live in these harsh conditions!

Small eyes for body size

Fangtooth ▼

A little fish with a very big mouth, this deep-sea hunter has the longest teeth in proportion to its size of any animal.

IF YOU THINK I LOOK COOL, YOU CAN BE IN MY FANG CLUB!

Bony spikes on head .....

Fangs so long it can't close its mouth .

Build it!

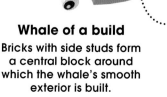

Blowhole is jumper plate

Curved slopes form curved sides

Whale of a build
Bricks with side studs form a central block around which the whale's smooth exterior is built.

Beaches and rock pools

Imagine if your home kept changing all day long, from bone dry to soaking wet and then back again. That's life for the creatures of the seashore as the tide flows in and out. Shoreline residents all have clever ways of adapting to their changing environment.

▼ Seaweed

There are thousands of different types of seaweed. Some grow like forests out of the seabed, and others are tiny and drift along in the water. Seaweed is an important food for all kinds of ocean animals.

Leaves are called blades and can be green, red, or brown

Some seaweeds have suckers to cling to rocks

Build it!

Crab core

The crab's legs and pincers clip onto an octagonal ring element in the center of its body. The head and shell sit on top.

Quarter dome piece

Feelers clip under edge of shell

Octagonal ring element

PINCERS ARE HANDY IF YOU HAVE TO FIGHT OVER A NEW HOME!

▼ Hermit crab

This crab can't grow a shell of its own, so it borrows one left behind by a sea snail or other shore creature. As hermits grow, they have to leave their home to find a new, bigger shell.

Feelers, called antennae, find food and other crabs

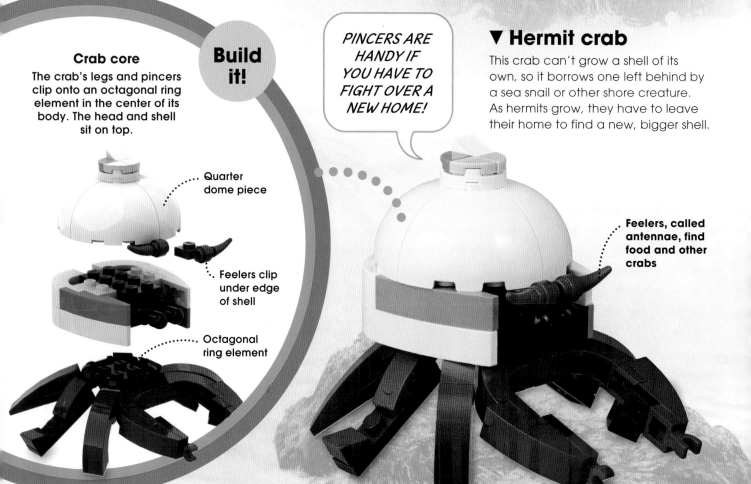

2x2 curved slope

1x1 headlight brick

1x1 round tile

Beady eye

Each of the gull's eyes is a printed 1x1 round tile mounted on a headlight brick. Gray, curved bricks above and behind the eyes form the bird's rounded head.

Build it!

IF I SEE SOMETHING TASTY, IT'S MINE!

Herring gull ▶

Gulls are the recyclers of the shore, swooping down on animals that have died or are stranded in rock pools. Watch out—sometimes they'll even steal your seaside snacks!

Webbed feet for swimming

Shrimp ▼

These small cousins of the lobster have soft shells. They paddle through the water with their tiny back legs, called swimmerets.

I MAY BE SMALL, BUT I'M A SPEEDY SWIMMER!

Shrimp feels its way with long antennae

Tail helps push the shrimp along

Habitat facts

The four main types of **beach** are **muddy**, **sandy**, **shingle** (small stones), and **rocky**. Animals and plants have to adapt to each type—from mussels that cling tightly to rocks, to crabs that can bury themselves in sand to hide from hungry gulls.

Gaping mouth in the middle of its body

Sea anemone ▶

Although it looks like a flower, the anemone is an animal that's part of the jellyfish family. Its long, stinging tentacles reach out to grab passing food, then transfer it into its mouth.

Sticky foot grips rock tightly

23

Coral reefs

A coral reef isn't just home to lots of living creatures, it's actually made of them! Corals look like rocks, but are really tiny animals with hard outer shells. They bind together under the sea to form colorful, rocky banks, like Australia's amazing Great Barrier Reef.

Habitat facts

In the **shallow waters** of a reef, tiny floating creatures, called **plankton**, provide food for many bigger fish. Some fish, such as the **manta ray**, have developed a clever way to eat tiny plankton. The ray's wide mouth **works like a sieve**, sucking in water, straining out the plankton, and spitting out the water again.

Stinging tail forces enemies to back off ....

Spotted eagle ray ▲

This fish flaps its wide fins to "fly" gracefully like an underwater bird. Its spotted body blends in perfectly when it hides on the rocky seabed, on the lookout for food.

Giant clam ▼

During the day, this supersize shellfish opens up so the sun can reach the algae growing inside it. The algae use the light to make food for the clam to eat. What a partnership!

Grows to more than 3 ft (1 m) wide .....

Build it!

1x2 plate with bar

1x8 plate

1x4 plate with clip

Open up

Clip-and-bar connections form hinges that give this clam its open shape. Long, white plates reinforce the build from behind.

..... **Clams can weigh up to 660 lb (300 kg)—more than 4 humans!**

Skin can change color to blend into surroundings .....

Slimy coating on skin protects clown fish from anemone stings

◀ Spiny seahorse

This tiny, spiny creature may not look like one, but it really is a fish! It uses its long, bendy snout to hunt and suck up plankton.

I MAY BE THE SLOWEST FISH IN THE WORLD, BUT I GET THERE IN THE END!

▲ Clown fish

Clown fish make their home among the stinging tentacles of a sea anemone. Clown fish keep the anemone clean and, in return, the anemone protects them from bigger fish.

Tail curls around plants and corals

Flipper fins

Pieces usually found on the feet of scuba-diving LEGO® minifigures are used from top to bottom on this seahorse build!

Minifigure flipper piece .....

1x1 plate with clip

Flat body can slip easily between pillars of coral

WHEN OTHER FISH GET TOO CLOSE, I GRUNT TO WARN THEM OFF!

Build it!

1x1 plate with bar

◀ Blue angelfish

Angelfish love coral reefs—the underwater boulders and caves give shelter from storms as well as plenty of places to hide from hungry predators.

Craggy corals provide hiding places for reef animals

Coral is made up of thousands of tiny animals called polyps .....

▲ Coral

Corals can be many different shapes, sizes, and colors. Some look like underwater trees and flowers, while others grow in spiky columns or delicate fan shapes.

Polar regions

Right at the top and bottom of our planet are two very chilly polar regions—the Arctic in the north and the Antarctic in the south. Even in these harsh, icy wastelands, a few of the world's hardiest plants and animals have found ways to survive and thrive.

Habitat facts

The **Arctic** is made up of **ocean** with **land** all around it, plus a huge **lump of ice** in the middle that never melts. The climate is not quite as cold and harsh as in the **Antarctic**, so more land animals, birds, and plants can make their home there.

▼ Polar bear

The biggest bear on the planet, the polar bear is brilliantly adapted to its world. Incredibly thick fur and an all-over layer of blubber keep bears cozy as they hunt seals over the ice or in the freezing sea.

White fur blends in with the ice and snow

Sharp claws are great at gripping the slippery ice

I CAN SNIFF OUT A SEAL, EVEN WHEN IT'S HIDING UNDER THE ICE!

Tusk can grow to 9 ft 10 in (3 m)

PEOPLE CALL ME THE UNICORN OF THE SEA!

Strong tail helps it dive down as deep as 0.9 miles (1.5 km)

Narwhal ▲

This whale has one big feature— a very long, thin tusk that's actually a giant tooth! Nobody knows exactly what this tusk is for, but only males can grow one.

Build it!

1x3 curved slope

1x2/1x2 angle plate

Sleek build

The narwhal's smooth sides are made of curved slopes and tiles, attached to the top half with angle plates.

1x2 tile

Antarctic (South)

Sharp beak for cracking shells

Long, slim wings

Wandering albatross ▲
The world's biggest seabird spends most of its life soaring high over the Southern Ocean. Each long-distance flight covers thousands of miles.

THE VIEW FROM UP HERE IS GREAT—AS LONG AS YOU LIKE LOOKING AT ICE, ICE, AND MORE ICE!

Habitat facts
The one thing a **penguin** never has to worry about is being eaten by a **polar bear**! Penguins only live in the **Southern Hemisphere** (half) of the planet, whereas polar bears live in the **Northern Hemisphere** around the cold Arctic territory.

A small iceberg that breaks away from a larger one is called a growler

Only 10% of an iceberg appears above the water

▲ Iceberg
These huge blocks of floating ice can get busy. Many sea creatures use them to take a rest—and this attracts lots of hungry hunters, such as whales.

WE PENGUINS HUDDLE TOGETHER FOR WARMTH!

Build it!

1x2 curved slope

2x2 printed tile

Horn piece

1x1 round plate with hole

1x1 brick with four side studs

Face of a penguin
The penguin's head is built around a 1x1 brick with four side studs. Eyes attach to the two sides and its beak is a black horn piece.

Short, tightly packed feathers keep out the cold

White rings around eyes are spec-tacular!

◄ Adélie penguin
Like all penguins, Adélies can't fly. Instead, they use their wings like flippers to "fly" underwater, then launch themselves back up on the ice like mini missiles!

Frozen tundra

The Arctic tundra is the chilly, remote land that lies around the icy Arctic Circle, right at the top of our planet. "Tundra" means "treeless lands," a perfect description for this cold, windy, dry habitat where it's hard work for plants and animals to survive.

▼ Lichen

Lichens aren't plants—they're a unique partnership of a fungus and plantlike material called algae. Lichens grow incredibly slowly—some take 100 years to grow just one millimeter (³⁄₆₄ in)!

Lichens come in a rainbow of bright colors ....

Lichens can even live on bare rocks ....

PEOPLE AROUND HERE CALL ME THE TUNDRA GHOST. I DON'T KNOW WHY!

▼ Arctic hare

In the snowy tundra, the Arctic hare's thick, white fur is great camouflage. During short summers when the snow melts, its fur turns a bit darker.

Soft feathers for silent, stealthy flight

◄ Snowy owl

With no trees to shelter in, this huge owl has to make a nest on the hard ground. It flies low, listening for lemmings scurrying under the snow, then dives to catch them!

Strong, sharp talons for seizing prey

Eyes on sides of the head can spot danger easily ....

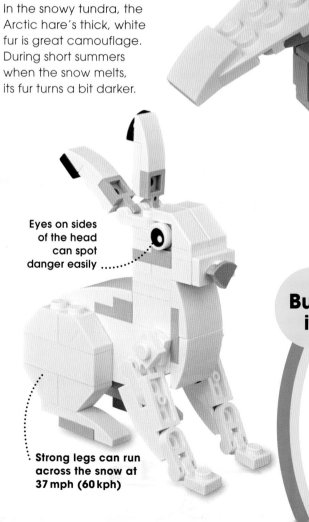

Strong legs can run across the snow at 37 mph (60 kph)

Build it!

2x4 wedge plate

1x2 plate with ball

2x2 curved slope

On the wing

Two wedge plates topped with a curved slope give the wing its elegant shape. A ball and socket joint allows for smooth movement.

Eclectic crown

These majestic antlers are made from an unexpected combination of LEGO elements and LEGO® Technic pieces in grays and browns.

Mechanical arm ·······

Bar holder with clip ·······

LEGO Technic T-bar

Build it!

Habitat facts

The **tundra** is treeless because summer doesn't last long enough for the ground to **thaw** properly. Under the surface, a thick layer of totally **frozen** soil called **permafrost** stops trees from putting down the **roots** they need to grow.

Reindeer ▶

This big, shaggy-coated deer uses its hard hooves and huge antlers to dig plants out of the frozen ground. Male reindeer also use their antlers as weapons to fight their rivals.

I SPEND MY LIFE ON THE MOVE WITH MY HERD!

Woolly coat has two layers for extra warmth

▼ Purple saxifrage

Summer in the tundra is very short, so as soon as the snow melts, this tough little plant bursts into life, producing a carpet of pretty pinkish-purple flowers.

Grows close to the ground to stay out of the icy wind

Hooves are wide so they don't sink into the snow ·····

Flowers are eaten by animals and local people

Bird-wing butterfly

Scarlet macaw

Poison dart frogs

Blue jay

Forests

When trees grow together, they make forests. Forests grow all over our planet, and whether they're hot and rainy, chilly and dry, or somewhere in between, they're home to more land animals than any other habitat.

Red deer

Forest habitats

Forests are essential for our planet. As well as being a leafy home for many animals, trees also make the oxygen that we all need to live. In rainforests, they even create their own rainclouds!

◀ Deciduous forests

Deciduous forests grow where the climate is neither too hot nor too cold. Many animals prefer this habitat because they can usually find enough to eat, even in winter.

▲ Coniferous forests

Although it's too cold for some animals, this is an ideal habitat for the birds and small mammals that feast on the cones and berries produced by the evergreen trees.

The forest floor ▶

Shady, cool, and damp, the forest floor is home to an army of woodland creatures, as well as colorful fungi and wild flowers.

Rainforests ▶

Among the tall, lush trees of the rainforest is a dazzling range of the most unusual, multi-colored plants and animals in the world. Bring your sunglasses!

◄ Rainforest insects

Deep in the Australasian rainforest, the insects are some of the biggest, buzziest, and most beautiful you'll ever see.

Deciduous forests

Some trees constantly change their outfits. In fall, they let their leaves drop off, then in spring they grow a new set of bright green leaves. These trees are called "deciduous," and their forests are a great place for animals to make their home.

Habitat facts

Why does wildlife love **deciduous** forests? The **soil** is super-rich and damp, so **plants** grow well. That means there's lots of **food** to go around—for the animals that eat the plants, and the animals that eat them! The forest is **warm** in summer, and in winter there's always a hidey-hole to **shelter** in, or to sleep in until spring comes.

I'LL GOBBLE UP ALMOST ANYTHING I FIND!

Huge eyes can spot the slightest movement

Hooked beak for tearing meat

◀ Tawny owl

An owl's round face acts like a satellite dish, collecting sound and directing it toward its ears. Handy if you're listening out for a mouse scuttling under dead leaves!

Curled-up frond unfurls as it grows

▲ Fern

Ferns grow well in the shady forest because the soil stays damp even in the heat of summer. They have large leaves, called fronds, to collect as much sunlight as possible.

Wild boar ▶

This pig uses his bendy snout to snuffle around for nuts, roots, worms, and small animals. A wild boar can weigh more than 660 lb (300 kg), so if it charges—watch out!

Sharp tusks for fighting off rivals

Legs are short and relatively thin for body size

Oak tree ▶

An oak tree is a mini habitat that can be home to hundreds of creatures. A single oak tree can produce up to 90,000 fruits, called acorns, a year. They provide food for many forest animals.

> BACK OFF! I'VE GOT ANTLERS AND I'M NOT AFRAID TO USE THEM!

···· **Only males have antlers**

In spring and summer, branches are covered in green leaves

Red-brown coat grows thicker in cooler seasons ····

Red deer ▶

The forest provides red deer with shelter from the weather and from predators and human hunters. They graze on grass and leaves in summer, but make do with bare twigs in winter.

Black woodpecker ▼

Insects hidden deep inside a tree? No problem for the woodpecker! It hammers out a hole in the hard wood, then sticks in its long tongue and slurps up the bugs.

Super-tough beak can hammer 20 times a second

Claws grip tree trunk ····

Build it!

1x1 round plate with hole

Unicorn horn ····

1x1 brick with side studs

Peck and mix

To make the woodpecker's strong beak, a unicorn horn piece is clipped into a 1x1 round plate with hole. Both are attached sideways to a 1x1 brick with 4 side studs.

Coniferous forests

Life is tough in a coniferous forest—so the trees have to be, too! Plants and animals have special features that help them survive long, harsh winters and make the most of the short warm season.

Build it!

Winging it

Build up a colorful, feathery wing using layers of thin plates and tiles attached to a brick with side studs in the bird's body.

3x3 angled plate

1x1 round quarter tile

Giant redwood ▶

Meet the largest tree on the planet. A giant redwood can grow over 330 ft (100 m) tall, with a trunk so wide that you could carve out a tunnel and drive a car right through it!

Super-thick bark

▼ Blue jay

These crafty crows have a clever trick—they copy the calls of predator birds. This scares away other birds so the jays can steal their food!

DO YOU WANT TO HEAR MY HAWK IMPRESSION?

Tough beak to crack open seed cases

Wide root system

◀ White spruce

This tough tree can survive even the worst winters. Its needles, cones, and seeds provide essential food for forest birds and animals such as grouse, hares, and mice.

Snow slips off sloping branches

Males grow new antlers every year

I'M A BRILLIANT SWIMMER!

◀ Moose

The world's biggest deer looks fierce, but is actually a shy plant-muncher. In winter, it can survive on tree bark and tough pine needles.

Habitat facts

Conifers like the redwood and spruce are also called **evergreens**, because instead of having leaves that drop off in the fall, their hard, green **needles** stay on all year. Their seeds grow in hard cases called **cones**—which is where the name "conifer" comes from.

Long, frost-proof fur

Build it!

1x1 slope

1x2 rounded plate

Face off
Small LEGO® pieces of all different shapes can be used to build up cute creature faces.

1x1 plate with clip

▲ Wolverine

Although they're from the same family as badgers, wolverines are bigger, stronger, and much, much fiercer. They even steal food from bears!

37

Forest floor

In cool forests, the floor is a thick carpet of fallen fruits and seeds, dead leaves, and rotting wood. All kinds of animals, bugs, bacteria, worms, and fungi come to enjoy this splendid feast.

▼ Bracket fungus

This hard fungus grows outward from dead tree trunks, just like a shelf. It provides valuable food for insects and bugs.

▼ White-lipped snail

Snails release a trail of silvery slime from their bodies, which helps them slide easily over the ground as they search for food.

Spiral shell protects soft body

Eyes on the end of tentacles

Grows on dead trunks and helps break them down

Can grow to 2 in (5 cm) long

Tough shell

DON'T MESS WITH MY MANDIBLES!

Stag beetle ▲

This bug is seriously big! It lives in fallen logs, and the males have massive jaws, called mandibles, that look just like a deer's antlers.

Hedgehog ▶

A hedgehog's sharp spines are actually specially adapted hairs. When it senses danger, it rolls up into a prickly ball—most predators don't want a mouthful of spikes!

Sensitive snout snuffles for insects

Up to 7,000 spines

HEY FRIEND, ARE YOU IN THERE?

Can curl up into a ball of spikes

Habitat facts

The **forest floor** is like a recycling station—everything gets **reused** in a never-ending circle of life. Rotting wood, leaves, and animal poo are **broken down** by tiny bacteria and insects. This process releases materials that seep into the soil and make **plants grow**, producing more **food** for the animals.

I LOVE TO EAT INSECTS CALLED APHIDS. I CAN EAT 50 A DAY!

▼ Ladybug

The ladybug's brightly colored shell and black spots are a warning message to predators—"Don't eat me, or you'll feel sick!"

Wings hidden under hard shell

Fly agaric toadstool ▼

Toadstools and mushrooms look like plants, but they are actually types of fungus. Fungi don't need sunlight to grow, so the damp, shady forest floor is their ideal home.

Red cap is poisonous!

Build it!

Stacked plates form curved shell

Antenna is a bar with round plate

Ladybug layers

The ladybug's face, legs, and shell attach to a central box, built on a 4x4 plate.

Robot arms clip onto octagonal ring

Rainforests

The hot, humid forests surrounding the mighty Amazon River in South America are home to a brain-boggling variety of squawking, growling, whooping, hissing wildlife. They also contain some of the tallest trees and most unusual plants on the planet.

▼ Scarlet macaw

These large, long-tailed parrots live way up in the highest trees, feeding on nuts and fruit. They use loud, screeching calls to find each other among the treetops.

Strong beak helps it climb trees

NUTS ARE MY FAVORITE FOOD!

Scarlet macaw has feathers of many colors

◄ Rainforest orchid

These beautiful plants grow high on tall trees, so they can grab some energy-giving sunlight. Most use their roots to absorb the moisture they need from the humid air.

Colorful petals attract insects

LEAVE US ALONE—OR YOU'LL BE SORRY!

◄ Poison dart frog

They may only be the size of an adult's fingernail, but these frogs are deadly—some species have enough poison on their skin to kill 10,000 mice!

Bright patterns warn predators not to eat them

Tilting head
Create a natural angle for your animal's head by using a hinge brick and plate. Attach the head centrally with a jumper plate.

2x2 jumper plate

Hinge brick and plate

Build it!

Fruit pods open to release pale, silky seed fibers

◀ Kapok tree
The kapok is one of the 6,000 different types of trees in the rainforest, and one of the tallest. It can live for more than 500 years!

Ocelot ▶
This forest feline is twice the size of a pet cat. It snoozes in the trees during the day, waking up to go hunting when it starts to get dark.

Rounded ears

Spotted coat is good camouflage among the forest leaves

HUH, THAT MACAW THINKS SHE'S A BIG NOISE AROUND HERE—BUT I'M MUCH LOUDER!

Large, thick roots grow out from the trunk to help keep it upright

◀ Red howler monkey
Howlers are officially the loudest of all land animals! Their booming barks can be heard for 3 miles (5 km), warning other groups to stay out of their territory.

Long tail helps with climbing

Habitat facts
Like the ocean, the **rainforest** has different layers, or **zones**, each providing a home for different plants and animals:

Emergent layer The highest level is where the tallest trees poke up toward the sky.
Canopy Tall treetops form a thick "roof" of leaves and branches.
Understory The next level down is made of shorter trees, bushes, and vines.
Forest floor Right at the bottom is a dark, damp layer of dead leaves and fallen fruits.

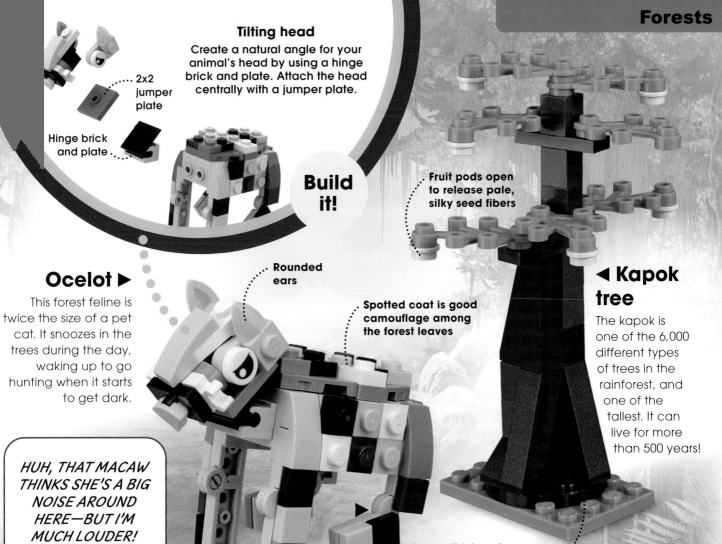

Rainforest insects

The rainforests in Australasia are a jumble of jungles—some are hot and steamy, while others are much cooler. But all of them are rainy and contain an awesome range of the world's creepiest, crawliest insects.

Praying mantis ▼

The mantis is a sneaky hunter. It waits, perfectly still, until a smaller insect gets close. Then, quick as a flash, it pounces on the prey and chomps down with strong jaws.

I'M PRAYING FOR PREY TO COME ALONG

Huge eyes to spot prey

◄ Bird-wing butterfly

The world's largest butterflies have a bigger wingspan than many rainforest birds. Their big, strong wings help them fly right up into the treetops to feed on climbing plants.

Proboscis sucks up nectar from plants

The butterfly's poison protects it from predators

Tough shell

Build it!

IF YOU'RE IN A STICKY SITUATION ... ACT LIKE A STICK!

Spiky, grabbing forelegs

Bar holder with handle

LEGO bar

Bar holder with clip

Stick and stack

The stick insect's jointed legs are made from LEGO bars connected by bar holders with handles and bar holders with clips.

▲ Giant prickly stick insect

Also called "the Australian walking stick," this giant bug is as long as your forearm. It hides from predators by looking almost exactly like the thorny twigs it rests on.

Camouflaged wings look like leaves

▲ Long-nosed lantern fly

It's easy to see how this bug got its name! It uses its long, hollow snout like a straw to suck the sweet sap from the trunks of trees.

Strong legs for jumping

Habitat facts

Rainforests are home to more types of **insects** than anywhere else in the world. There are so many that scientists believe there are **thousands of species** that have not even been **discovered** yet! The constant **rain** means plants can grow **all year**—providing an all-you-can-eat buffet for millions of hungry bugs.

◄ Monkey cup pitcher

This meat-eating plant has a cunning way of catching prey. Insects land on the slippery rim of a jug-shaped leaf, then tumble down into a pool of liquid inside. There's no escape! The plant is named after the thirsty monkeys that are able to drink safely from its pitchers.

Pitcher plants are climbers that grow on trees

Water collects inside the cups

HELP! I'M STUCK INSIDE THIS PLANT!

43

Meerkat

Roadrunner

Desert tortoise

Horned viper

Argali

Snow leopard

Mountains and lowlands

Over millions of years, huge chunks of the Earth's surface have pushed against each other, forcing the ground up to make towering mountains surrounded by vast, open lowlands.

Mountain and lowland habitats

On the Earth's highest spots, life is cold and harsh. But for the wildlife that goes low instead, it might get so hot that they need to take cover!

▼ High mountains

On the slopes of the world's high mountains, the ground is icy and rocky and there's little shelter from extreme weather. Only the toughest animal mountaineers live here.

▲ Cool, dark caves

Deep, rocky caves set in the mountainside give shelter from cold, rain, and snow, and safety from predators. You'd better not be scared of the dark, though ...

Grasslands ▶

The African plains attract all kinds of grass-eating wildlife. Some of the planet's fiercest predators know this, too—so watch out, they're on the hunt!

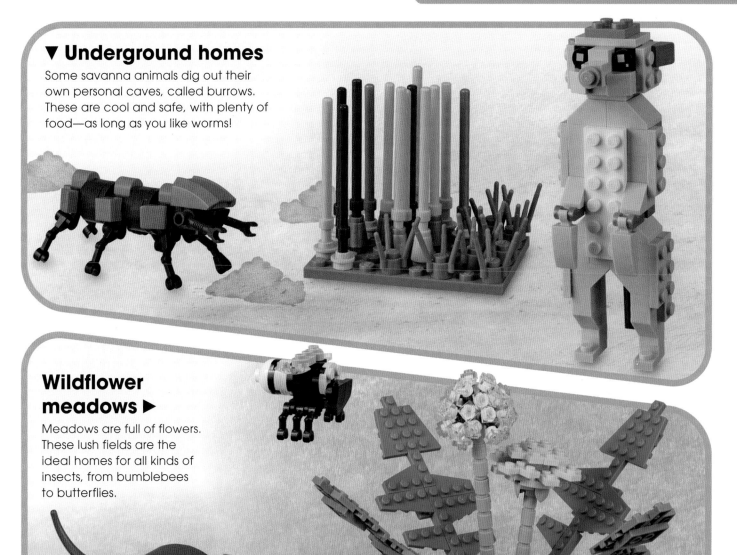

▼ Underground homes

Some savanna animals dig out their own personal caves, called burrows. These are cool and safe, with plenty of food—as long as you like worms!

Wildflower meadows ▶

Meadows are full of flowers. These lush fields are the ideal homes for all kinds of insects, from bumblebees to butterflies.

▲ Deserts

In the fierce heat of the day, a sandy desert can look empty and lifeless. But look closer—there's plenty of life if you know where to search.

▼ Desert at night

One of the ways to survive the desert heat is to live by the light of the moon. Watch out, though—it gets colder than you might think!

Life on the mountain

On the Himalayan mountains, wildlife faces the same challenges as a human mountaineer—the higher you go, the colder it gets, and the less oxygen there is to breathe. But even here, in the highest habitat on Earth, life can survive and thrive.

UH-OH! IS THAT A ROCK OR A SNOW LEOPARD?

Build it!

Argali ▼

The world's largest wild sheep also has the biggest, fanciest horns! Although they look threatening, argalis live in peaceful herds, chomping grass and drinking melted snow on the high slopes.

Three layers of fur to keep out the cold

Long legs for climbing steep, rocky crags

Big, brightly colored flowers attract insects and birds

Waxy leaves hold in moisture

Blooming brick

A brick with side studs connects to multiple flower buds and plates with bars. Leaves clip onto these bars, allowing them to be angled.

Brick with side studs

Plate with bar

▲ Wild rhododendron

These tree-size plants grow in huge forests in mountain valleys. Their tough leaves are poisonous, which is great protection against being eaten by hungry animals!

48

Bar holder with clip

Elephant tail piece

1x2 plate with bar

Tall tail

A bar holder with handle clips onto a plate with bar creating a movable tail.

Build it!

Habitat facts

At the top of **Mount Everest**, temperatures can reach –76°F (–60°C) and there are **hurricane-force winds**. No plants or animals can live there. But scientists have found that a type of **bacteria** called a psychrophile may be able to survive—because it produces **antifreeze** molecules inside its **body**.

Long tail helps it balance as it climbs

I'M NOT HANGING AROUND TO FIND OUT!

Sharp claws for climbing

▲ Red panda

This cute critter isn't a panda at all—it's a relative of the raccoon. Perfectly adapted for life in the trees, it can twist its feet around and climb down a tree-trunk head first!

Blotchy coat gives camouflage against snow and rocks

Leaves are small and needlelike

◀ Juniper tree

Junipers are brilliantly adapted to their surroundings. They are short, to avoid being battered by the wind; they don't need much water; and with their deep roots they can stay stable even on the rockiest slopes.

Thick bark keeps water inside the trunk

◀ Snow leopard

Furry paw-pads for walking on snow

This beautiful cat is perfectly made for the cold. Its fur is extra thick, and at night it wraps its tail around its body, like a super-cozy scarf.

Rock caves

If our planet were an apartment building, caves would be the basement level. They're very dark and the air can be stuffy. On the plus side, they usually have a good water supply and they never get too hot or cold. For some animals, a cave is the ultimate luxury home!

Water drips down to form stalactites

Spikes that form upward from the ground are called stalagmites

▲ Stalactites

When water drips very, very slowly from a cave's roof, eventually the minerals in the water harden and form these downward-pointing, rocky spikes.

Eyes are covered in scales

MY FAVORITE MEAL IS BAT POO. TRUST ME, IT'S YUMMY!

Leathery, segmented body

Colorless skin

Giant cave cockroach ▶

The world's biggest cockroach uses its antennae and leg bristles to feel its way around its dark, damp home. Its flat body is ideal for nestling in cracks and crevices.

▲ Blind cave fish

This little fish has adapted to life in dark underground waters by losing its eyes altogether. It finds it way by feeling vibrations through special nerves on the sides of its body.

Build it!

1x1 brick with side studs

1x1 plate with handle

Fin is 1x2 curved slope

Fish stack

This fish is built from its tail up. A 1x1 brick with side studs provides a place to attach its fins.

Hinged plate

2x4 wedge plate

1x1 plate with clip

Folding wings

The bat's movable wings are built with two hinged plates and two wedge plates each.

Build it!

Habitat facts

Caves are useful to all kinds of **animals**! Some are so adapted to cave life that they couldn't survive in the **outside** world. Others, such as bats, go out every night to **find food**, then **return** to their cave to rest. But many other animals, such as rats, bears, and raccoons, use caves as a **temporary** home, or to escape danger or bad weather.

Bat ▶

Instead of using their eyesight, bats find their way by making squeaking noises, then listening for echoes as the noises bounce off objects. Bats can even find tiny, fast-flying insects using this clever navigation tool.

> BATMAN ISN'T THE ONLY ONE WHO LIVES IN A BAT CAVE, YOU KNOW!

Wings made of stretchy flaps of skin

Yellow-red rat snake ▶

To this small snake, caves mean yummy bats, and lots of them! It slithers up a cave wall and dangles from a crack in the ceiling, waiting to grab a bat as it flies by.

> AH, GREETINGS-S-S-S, BAT.

Reddish or brown spots

Green, sparkly glow

◀ Cave moss

Some mosses can still grow where light is very faint, such as near the entrance to a cave. They can even reflect some of this light and glow in the dark!

Grassland animals

What grows in a place that's rainier than a desert, but not wet enough for trees to grow? The answer is grass! In Africa, grasslands are called savannas. Some of the planet's biggest land animals live here, so let's go on safari and spot some.

Leaves drop off in the dry season to save water

▲ Baobab tree

On the savanna, the lack of rain makes it tough for trees to survive. The baobab has an extra-thick trunk that swells up even more when it rains, storing water for the dry season.

EVERY DAY, I MAKE A PILE OF POO THAT WEIGHS MORE THAN YOU!

MY COUSIN ZAZU IS A FAMOUS MOVIE STAR.

Extra-strong neck helps support large bill

Red-billed hornbill ▶

This bird's big, curved bill is the perfect tool for digging beetles, grasshoppers, termites, and lizards out of the sun-baked ground of the savanna.

Long teeth called tusks

Thick, wrinkled skin helps it stay cool

▲ African elephant

The savanna's biggest animal can weigh 13,000 lb (6,000 kg)—that's more than 75 people! To keep cool in the fierce sun, the elephant flaps its enormous ears like giant fans.

Build it!

1x2 jumper plate

Packed trunk

A long, curved trunk attaches to jumper plates on the elephant's face. The trunk is made from curved slopes and bricks.

1x4 curved slope

Umbrella-shaped
branches and
leaves

▲ Acacia tree

Animals love to munch the
acacia's tasty leaves—but
the trees hit back with spiky
thorns that are as long as a
banana. Only the giraffe's
long tongue can reach
around these spines.

*HUH! A FEW
THORNS
WON'T PUT
ME OFF MY
LUNCH!*

*WHO WANTS TO
RACE ME? I'LL
GIVE YOU A HEAD
START!*

Spotted
markings for
camouflage
when hunting

Long, strong tail helps
with changing direction

▲ Cheetah

Whooooosh! This streamlined
feline is the fastest runner on
the planet. Its super-bendy
backbone means it can
stretch its long legs out
to reach maximum speed.

**Build
it!**

Head for heights

The giraffe's head attaches to its
long, angled neck using a hinge
brick and plate. Sloped bricks below
add stability to the connection.

1x2 jumper
plate

1x1 slope

2x2 hinge
brick and
plate

Patterned coat
is different for
every giraffe

◀ Giraffe

Everything about the
giraffe is long—even its
20 in (50 cm) tongue is
longer than your arm!
Its blue-black tongue is
tough and bendy, to
slither around thorny
branches.

Legs can be
6 ft (1.8 m) long

Habitat facts

On the **savanna**, **plant-eaters**
like zebras and wildebeests come
to eat the grass. They are hunted
by fierce **meat-eaters** like the
lion and cheetah. Afterward,
scavengers like jackals and vultures
feast on unfinished meat. Lastly,
decomposers—insects, bacteria,
and fungi—feed on whatever
remains, turning it into **nutrients**
which make the **grass grow**—and
the whole cycle **starts again**!

Underground homes

For small savanna animals life above ground is risky, so many of them choose to go underground. A burrow provides shelter from the hot sun and cold nights, a hiding place from hungry predators, and plenty of tasty insects to snack on!

Meerkat ▼

Meerkats live together in big dens called burrows. They stand on their hind legs so they can spot danger and also to warm their bodies in the sun after coming up from underground.

Dark rings of fur act like sunglasses

DID YOU HEAR THAT? SOUNDED LIKE TROUBLE!

Sharp claws for digging

Ear flaps close up when digging

QUICK! TO THE BURROWS!

◀ Springhare

This little rodent makes giant hops, like a mini kangaroo! When it enters its burrow, it kicks up loose earth to close up the entrance and keep out nosy neighbors.

Powerful back legs

Build it!

1x4 curved slope

Brick with side stud

1x1 round plate

Ears to attention

A 1x1 round plate between the ear and the head allows the ear to be positioned in a variety of expressive angles.

Aardvark ▼

This odd-looking animal is perfectly adapted for hunting insects. It finds a nest with its snuffly nose, digs it out with strong claws, then slurps up the insects with its long, sticky tongue.

I CAN DIG A HOLE FASTER THAN ANYONE AROUND HERE!

Long ears fold down for digging ·······

Habitat facts

In all kinds of habitats, animals live in **underground homes**—tarantulas, tortoises, and toads, to name a few! A mother polar bear will dig a **burrow** in the **snow** to have her babies. When a **wombat** is in danger, it dives into its **burrow** face-first and blocks the **entrance** with its hard-skinned bottom!

Nostrils and mouth at end of long snout ·····

Long, segmented body ·······

◄ Termite

These insects mix earth with their spit and poo to build huge mounds—some as tall as three adult humans! The mounds keep the termite group inside sheltered from the blazing sun.

▼ Tall grass

Above ground, tall grass provides shelter for birds and animals but can also hide lurking predators.

····· **Grows up to 10 ft (3 m) tall**

Build it!

······ **2x2 curved slope often used on engines**

Robot arm piece ·····

Robotic worker

LEGO® pieces normally used for robots and mechanical objects are used here for insect legs and pincers.

····· **Battle droid arm piece**

Wildflower meadow

Meadows are fields filled with wild flowers, grasses, and herbs. A huge number of species nest, breed, and pollinate in meadows. Many of the plants and animals that live there could not survive anywhere else.

Flower head is actually thousands of separate flowers

I USE MY ANTENNAE TO TOUCH, SMELL, AND TASTE.

◀ Oxeye daisy

This plant is small, but its center is jam-packed with tiny, nectar-filled flowers, making it irresistible to butterflies and bees.

Ears are on the side of their body

◀ Grasshopper

This bug has very talented legs! Grasshoppers can jump more than 10 times their body length, but they also "sing" to each other by rubbing their legs and wings together.

Powerful hind legs

IN WINTER I FLUTTER OFF TO FIND SOME SUN!

Leg steps

The grasshopper's rear leg connects to the body using a LEGO Technic pin, allowing it to move backward and forward.

Build it!

LEGO® Technic pin

1x2 brick with hole

1x2 plate with ring

Orange-red wings

Red admiral butterfly ▲

This big beauty lays its eggs on stinging nettles—which might mean the eggs have a better chance of hatching before being gobbled up by hungry animals!

Builder bee

This bee is buzzing in all directions! Bricks with side studs sit in the center of the body and attach to the head, wings, tail, and legs.

1x2 brick with side studs ....

Upside-down plate with bar

Robot arms with clips make legs ....

Build it!

Wings can beat up to 240 times per second!

◀ Bumblebee

These insects visit flowers to find nectar and pollen to feed on. Their hairy bodies keep them warm, so bumblebees can live in cooler habitats than many other bees.

FLOWERS LIKE ME BECAUSE I SPREAD THEIR POLLEN AROUND AND HELP THEM GROW!

Dandelion ▶

Without the wind, there would be no dandelions. The flower head turns into a ball of seed-filled fluff. Then, when the wind blows, the seeds are carried far away to grow in a new patch of land.

Fuzzy seed head ....

Yellow flowers attract bees

Pollen sticks to hairy body

Jagged leaves ....

▼ Dormouse

When it's cold and there's no food around, the dormouse saves energy by simply going to sleep! It makes a ball-shape nest out of grass and snoozes until the sun comes out!

Fluffy tail keeps it warm while sleeping ....

Habitat facts

Long ago, most of Europe was covered in thick forest, but over time farmers **cleared away the trees, creating grassy fields**, or meadows. Some meadows are still managed by humans. These **hay meadows** are mowed regularly to provide animal feed.

Big eyes for finding food at night ....

Desert life

In the southwestern US, the desert is scorching hot and incredibly dry—some parts get just 2½ in (6 cm) of rain a year—not enough to fill a glass! All living things need water to survive, so animals and plants have developed cunning ways to make the most of the water they get.

Spikes stop thirsty animals from nibbling stems

I CAN RUN AS FAST AS A HUMAN OLYMPIC SPRINTER!

▲ Saguaro cactus

The biggest cactus in North America has a super-spongy stem that swells up to store water when it rains. A newly topped-up cactus can survive for a whole year without more rain!

Roadrunner ▶

This little bird can fly, but prefers to race over the desert chasing lizards and snakes. After a cold night, it fluffs its feathers and soaks up the sun through dark skin on its back.

Sharp beak for pecking prey

IT WAS LOVELY AND COOL UNDERGROUND!

Tough shell

Long toes for faster running

Minifigure neck bracket

Brick with two side studs

Build it!

Flat feet scoop out burrows

Stud solution

A minifigure neck bracket can be a good way of adding a side stud to a brick without one, or where you would like to add another.

▲ Desert tortoise

Keeping cool is at the top of the desert tortoise's "to do" list. It only comes out of its underground burrow at dawn or dusk, when the sun is not as hot.

Joshua tree ▶

In Spanish, the Joshua tree is called "the desert dagger" because of its long, spiky leaves. These store water, and have a special waxy coating to help keep the moisture in.

Thin, waxy leaves don't dry out

Habitat facts

Have you heard of **hibernation**, when some animals sleep right through the **cold winter**? Well, in the desert the **opposite** happens! Animals like the ground squirrel snooze through the hottest part of **summer**, when no plants can grow so there's nothing to eat. This hot-weather habit is called **estivation**.

Spread-out roots suck up rainwater

Long tail helps it climb

HEY TORTOISE, IS THERE ROOM FOR TWO IN YOUR BURROW?

◀ Round-tailed ground squirrel

If this little rodent doesn't feel like digging its own home, it uses an old tortoise burrow instead. When the sun is hottest, it escapes the burning-hot sand by climbing up into a bush.

I DIG MYSELF A HOME WITH MY SPADE-LIKE FEET.

Strong back legs for burrowing

Skin is covered in small warts

Toad legs

Attach the toad's leg at an angle, using hinged plates in the toad's underbelly. You can then build up the body and legs separately with plates and curved slopes.

1x2 curved slope

Hinged plates

1x2 inverted curved slope

Build it!

▲ Couch's spadefoot toad

The spadefoot spends most of its time underground. The minute it rains, it lays eggs. The tadpoles must hatch and change into toads before the water dries up—so they do it in less than two weeks!

Desert at night

When we think of the Sahara Desert, most of us imagine blazing sun and hot, rippling sand. But at night, the temperature can drop well below freezing. Desert residents need to be able to cope with both extremes, which is not as easy as it sounds!

Tall leaves soak up sunlight ......

Up to 1,000 fruits per bunch

◀ Date palm

This tough tree is an expert in desert survival. It sucks up underground water through its many roots, then stores it in its trunk, which it keeps cool with a crown of spiky leaves.

Hairy body traps grains of sand for camouflage ...

Long, sharp tail-tip injects poison into prey

The sand spider has the most potent spider venom

▲ Sand spider

Camouflage is the secret weapon this hunter uses to sneak up on insects and scorpions. It lurks in the sand, then pounces and sinks in its venomous fangs.

WATER IS FOR WIMPS. THE JUICY FLESH OF MY PREY IS ALL I NEED!

Build it!

1x4 curved double slope

2x4 plate

Plate with bar

Shell casing

The scorpion's legs and pincers are all attached using clips. These connect to plates with bars sandwiched between layers of long plates.

▲ Scorpion

This poisonous predator can go for months without food or water. It hunts at night, grabbing prey in powerful pincers and paralyzing it with a venomous sting.

◀ Oasis

An oasis is a place in the desert where water comes up from under ground. People can keep animals or grow plants that wouldn't usually survive in the desert, such as this olive tree.

Olive trees often have twisted trunks

Build it!

Flat ears

The fennec fox's big, flat ears are attached to the head using plates with clips. Small plates with bars are built into the ears.

Plate with bar

Plate with clip

MY SUPERSIZE EARS HELP ME LISTEN FOR MICE IN THE SAND.

Jerboa ▼

It looks like the world's smallest kangaroo, but it's really a kind of rat! When it's being chased, the jerboa hops in zig-zag patterns across the sand, to confuse predators.

6 in (15 cm) ears

Sand-colored fur for camouflage

Strong back legs can leap up to 10 ft (3 m)

I'M A RAT, NOT A 'ROO!

▲ Fennec fox

During the day, its enormous ears give out lots of body heat to help this fox stay cool. And for night wear, its bushy tail acts like a cozy scarf!

Horned viper ▼

This poisonous hunter ripples over the sand in a sideways "S" shape. This way of moving means that less of the snake's body touches the burning-hot sand.

Horns are sticking-up scales that keep the sand out of its eyes

Habitat facts

Darkness means **dinner**! The desert floor is often busier at night than during the day, when many creatures **shelter** from the fierce heat. After dark, small rodents creep out of their **burrows** to look for seeds and insects. They must stay alert for **danger** because predators like foxes, owls, and snakes are also wide **awake** and very hungry, too!

Meet the builders

The models in this book were designed and created by a talented team of builders who love building with LEGO® bricks and pieces! We asked them to share some of their thoughts about building LEGO models.

Jason Briscoe

What was your favorite animal build for this book?
The polar bear, although only a small build, has a pleasing look. It was one of the models that seemed to just go together the first time without too much revision. I think having so few studs on show helps make it look more appealing, too. The seagull (p.23) comes a close second.

What's your favorite animal in real life?
Currently I'd have to say ducks. I have a pair of white Aylesbury ducks called Doodle and Buddy and they are very amusing pets!

What's the most useful brick in your collection?
Such a tough question, as every year so many new cool elements are introduced! However, the new 1x2x2 multifaceted SNOT (Studs Not On Top) brick is proving very useful. It's often hidden inside my builds as it allows building on four of its six sides.

What other things do you like to build?
Like Benny from THE LEGO® MOVIE™, I love spaceships, spaceships, SPACESHIPS! I'm always building different ones.

What's the most challenging thing you've ever built?
Not surprisingly, a giant moon base and space docking port for spaceships.

Polar bear

Nate Dias

What was your favorite animal build for this book?

This was a really tough choice, but my favorite has to be the dormouse. It's just so cute! For such a small build, there's a lot of character in its adorable little face. Also, it's one of only a few of my designs that do not have any studs showing, giving the appearance of a smooth coat.

What's your favorite animal in real life?

I have to say a mole. I've loved them since being in elementary school. It's amazing how strong they are for their size and I love that there are so many of them all around us, despite most of us never actually seeing one. Like little garden ninjas!

What's the most useful brick in your collection?

For this book, it has been the 1x2 curved slope. They help create some lovely, organic shapes, which is really helpful when we are recreating natural things out of plastic bricks!

What other things do you like to build?

Real-life objects. I love to make everyday items out of LEGO bricks and then hide them in plain sight. Recently I did this with some exotic plants that I made out of LEGO bricks, which were displayed in one of the glasshouses of the Royal Horticultural Society (RHS).

What's the most challenging thing you've ever built?

A 6½ ft x 6½ ft (2 m x 2 m) life-size man sitting at his desk with his inner child (who had escaped and was playing happily). I built this with my friend, Steve. It helped us win the first LEGO® MASTERS series.

Dormouse

Jessica Farrell

What was your favorite animal build for this book?

The red deer was most enjoyable. I loved selecting the perfect color blend and shaping the graceful body so that it looked both strong and delicate, just like a real deer.

What's your favorite animal in real life?

Goats! They are so cute, friendly, and playful! I also admire how agile and hardy they can be.

What's the most useful brick in your collection?

The jumper plate. It enables fine detailing by allowing you to offset elements by half a stud. I once built a model that used almost 7,000 jumper plates!

What other things do you like to build?

Everything! I try to vary my work as much as possible so I am always learning and meeting new challenges.

What's the most challenging thing you've ever built?

A five-floor London department store. It was 9 ft (2.7 m) long, used 105,282 pieces, and took a year to create!

Red deer

Useful bricks

Brick basics

Bricks are the basis of most LEGO® builds. They come in many shapes and sizes, and are named according to size.

2x3 brick overhead view

2x3 brick side view

Plates are the same as bricks, only slimmer. Three stacked plates are the same height as a standard brick.

1x2 plate

3 1x2 plates   **1x2 brick**

Tiles look like plates, but without any studs on top. This gives them a smooth look for more realistic builds.

2x2 tile   **2x2 round tile**

1x6 tile

Slopes are any bricks with diagonal angles. They can be big, small, curved, or inverted (upside-down).

1x2 slope   **1x2 inverted slope**

1x3 curved slope

Cool connectors

Jumper plates allow you to "jump" the usual grid of LEGO studs. Use them to center things like flags or other decorations.

1x2 jumper plate

There are different kinds of **bricks with side studs**. They all allow you to build outward as well as upward.

1x1 brick with two side studs   **1x2/2x2 angle plate**

Plates with sockets and **plates with balls** link together to make flexible connections for things like wings and legs.

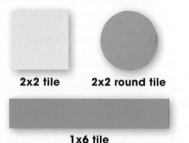

1x2 plate with ball   **1x2 plate with socket**

Any piece with a **bar** can fit onto a piece with a **clip**. Use clips and bars to make moving or angled features.

1x2 plate with bar   **1x1 plate with clip**

Hinge plates can give your builds side-to-side movement. **Hinge bricks** are used to tilt things up and down.

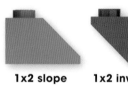

Hinge plates   **1x2 hinge brick with 2x2 hinge plate**

LEGO® Technic parts expand the range of functions you can build into your models.

LEGO Technic beam

LEGO Technic friction pin

Ears

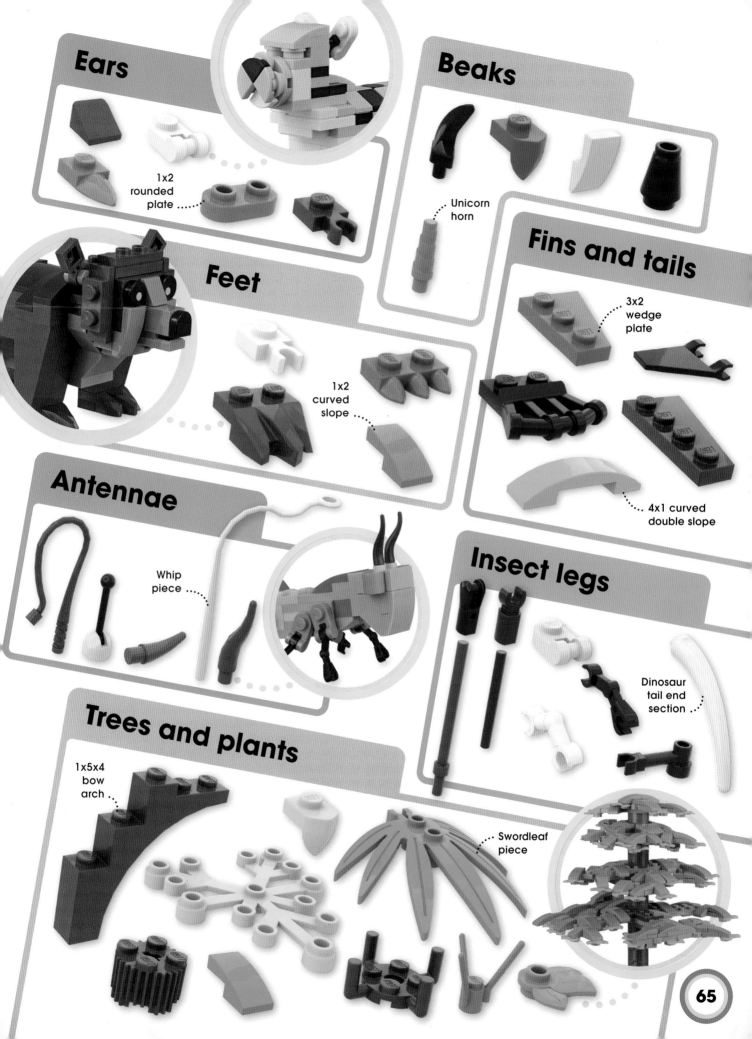

1x2 rounded plate ......

Beaks

Unicorn horn ....

Feet

1x2 curved slope ......

Fins and tails

3x2 wedge plate ....

4x1 curved double slope ....

Antennae

Whip piece ......

Insect legs

Dinosaur tail end section ....

Trees and plants

1x5x4 bow arch ....

Swordleaf piece ....

Glossary

Adaptation
The way a species of animal changes, over many years, to survive better. For example, the giraffe has adapted to eat the leaves of tall trees by developing a super-long neck.

Algae
Simple plants that grow in water. Seaweeds are a type of algae.

Amphibians
A family of animals that can live easily both on land and in water. Frogs and newts are types of amphibian.

Animals
Living creatures that breathe air, eat and drink, move around, and have babies.

Antennae
A pair of long, thin feelers on the head. Some animals, especially insects, use antennae to smell, touch, or hear.

Antlers
Bony, branching horns on the heads of deer. Every year they fall off and new antlers grow.

Bacteria
Very tiny, simple life forms. They live almost everywhere on Earth, even inside our bodies!

Birds
A family of animals with wings, feathers, and beaks. Most birds can fly. Macaws and owls are birds.

Blubber
A thick layer of fat under the skin. Whales and polar bears have lots of blubber to keep them warm in the cold ocean.

Camouflage
A color or pattern on fur or skin that blends in with an animal's surroundings, helping it hide.

Climate
The normal weather you can expect in a place over a period of time.

Continents
Huge areas of land: the seven continents are Europe, Africa, Asia, North America, South America, Australasia, and Antarctica.

Coral
When millions of tiny undersea animals called polyps grow hard skeletons and bunch together, they form rocky structures called coral reefs.

Desert
A bare, dry area that has less than 9⅞ in (25 cm) of rain a year. Deserts can be hot, like the Sahara, or cold, like the Antarctic.

Environment
A living thing's surroundings.

Fish
A type of animal that lives only in water. Fish breathe through slits called gills, and have fins to help them swim. Tuna and rays are fish.

Flower
The part of a plant with petals. Flowers are often colorful to attract insects to gather and spread the pollen they make.

Fungus
A plantlike type of living thing that feeds mainly on dead animals and plants. Mushrooms are a type of fungus.

Grasses
A family of plants with long, thin leaves and round stems. Wheat and bamboo are types of grass.

Habitat
The place where an animal or plant usually lives – its natural home.

Insects
Small animals with six legs, a tough shell, and a three-part body. Most insects also have wings. Flies, bees, and ants are insects.

Invertebrates
Animals with no backbone such as insects, crabs, and worms.

Mammals
Animals that make milk to feed their babies and have hair on their skin. Mice, cats, and humans are mammals.

Mosses
Short plants with no flowers, which spread out slowly and grow in damp, shady places.

Nectar
A sweet syrup that flowers make to attract insects such as bees. In return, bees help plants reproduce (make new plants).

North and South Poles
Points at the very top and bottom of our planet, and the regions around them (the Arctic and Antarctic). The poles are very cold and icy.

Oxygen
An invisible gas that's in air and water. Animals breathe in oxygen to make energy. Without oxygen, there would be no life on Earth.

Plankton
Tiny plants and animals that drift in oceans, lakes, and rivers. Some whales feed on plankton.

Plants
Living things, mostly with stems and leaves. They take in water with their underground roots. Plants cannot move around like animals can.

Pollen
A powder made by plants, which helps make new plants. Often, animals like bees help by taking pollen from one plant to another.

Polyps
Tiny animals that live in the sea. They grow hard outer shells and cling together to make coral.

Predator
An animal that hunts other animals for food. Orcas and owls are predators.

Prey
An animal that is hunted by another for food. Mice are the prey of owls.

Rainforest
An area that gets lots of rain, allowing a thick forest of trees to grow. Although most rainforests are hot, they can be cool, too.

Reptiles
A type of animal with a body covered with scales or bony armor. Snakes and tortoises are reptiles.

Rodents
A type of mammal that has extra-strong front teeth for gnawing. Mice, hares, and squirrels are all rodents.

Rotting
Decaying or breaking down into parts. Rotting happens to all living things after they die.

Seed
A small, living part of a plant which falls off and grows into a new plant.

Species
A group of animals of the same type. Its males and females can have babies together.

Tentacles
Long, bendy arms used for grabbing and feeding.

Tree
A big plant that lives for a long time. Trees have a tough, woody trunk and branches. Most trees have leaves.

Red-billed hornbill

Venom
A poison made by an animal. A venomous animal uses poisonous bites or stings to catch prey or fight enemies.

Index

Monkey cup pitcher

Long-nosed lantern fly

Sand spider

Horned viper

Meerkat

Argali

Rhododendron